Award-Winning Sports Broadcasters

CRIS COLLINSWORTH

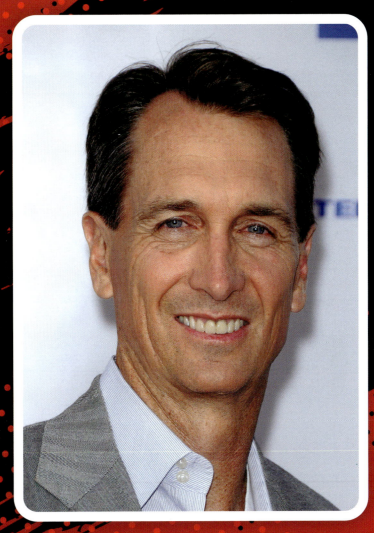

Tammy Gagne

Mitchell Lane

PUBLISHERS

2001 SW 31st Avenue
Hallandale, FL 33009
www.mitchelllanepub.com

Copyright © 2025 by Mitchell Lane Publishers. All rights reserved. No part of this book may be reproduced without written permission from the publisher. Printed and bound in the United States of America.

First Edition, 2025.
Author: Tammy Gagne
Designer: Ed Morgan
Editor: Morgan Brody

Series: Award-Winning Sports Broadcasters
Title: Cris Collinsworth

Hallandale, FL : Mitchell Lane Publishers, [2025]

Library bound ISBN: 979-8-89260-073-6
eBook ISBN: 979-8-89260-078-1

PHOTO CREDITS: cover, title page, 11, 19, 25, 27, 29, 30, 35, 37, 38, 41 Alamy; p. 5, 14 Freepik.com; p. 7 flickr.com All-Pro Reels; p. 13, 17, 20 wikimedia; p. 23, 32-33, newscom.com;

CONTENTS

1. **An Expert** on the **Game** 4
2. **Son** of a **Basketball Player** 10
3. From a **Quarterback** to a **Top Wide Receiver** 18
4. **Best Laid Plans** 26
5. *Sunday Night Football* 34

Timeline 42
Find Out More 43
Glossary 44
Works Consulted 46
Index 48
About the Author 48

CHAPTER ONE

AN EXPERT on the GAME

"Welcome to the Great Debate, where the ride goes fast because everyone gets a turn to talk. I'm Mr. Vasquez, your dapper host and devoted school bus driver. What shall our topic be today?"

Scarlet and Carter smiled as the other students shouted their suggestions. They all adored Mr. V and the pretend game show he invented for their ride home each afternoon. Everyone knew it began as a ploy to get everyone to behave well and keep the volume reasonable. But it was so much fun, they didn't care.

CHAPTER **ONE**

"How about the Brotherly Shove?" Carter asked. He was an avid football fan and had seen the Philadelphia Eagles perform the play many times. It involved players pushing the **quarterback** forward to make it harder for the opposing team to stop him. Some people thought the play was a genius sports strategy. Others believed it should be banned.

"Ooh, that's a good one," Mr. V decided. "Which side are you on, Carter? And be sure to support your argument."

"I'm in favor of it," Carter stated. "There is no rule against it, and it is remarkably effective."

"Scarlet, you're up. What say you?" Mr. V asked.

"I'm against it," she countered. "It's not a football play. It's something better suited to rugby."

After allowing several more students to chime in on the issue, Mr. V switched gears. "Alright," he announced, "I think it's time to weigh some expert advice. Has anyone read any good articles about the play? I'm looking for quotes here. Who has the fastest thumbs on the Google app?"

AN EXPERT on the GAME

Tight end Dallas Goedert and quarterback Jalen Hurts (left to right) started performing the Brotherly Shove with their Philadelphia Eagles teammates in 2022.

CHAPTER ONE

"Jason Kelce says, 'Ban it,'" a student toward the back shared. "I just read that on the *Bleacher Report*." Mr. V insisted that students provide their sources for this part of the game.

"You're taking that comment out of **context**," another student pointed out. "Kelce said he is tired of talking about the play, so he just doesn't care if it's banned. He doesn't think the Eagles need it to win games."

"Anyone have a quote from an unbiased expert?" Mr. V then asked. During other debates, he had explained that being unbiased meant dealing with just the facts and not favoring one side or another.

"Cris Collinsworth has talked about the safety concerns," Scarlet said as she scrolled through an online article. "He told the *Today Show*, 'You've got a lot of players lowering their heads—the centers, the guards, the defensive linemen—trying to get underneath other players.'" She then added, "Collinsworth is an NFL announcer as well as a former player. I think that makes him an unbiased expert in two ways."

AN EXPERT on the GAME

"But aren't you biased because you're such a Collinsworth fan?" Carter asked. Scarlet couldn't deny that she greatly admired the sports broadcaster. In addition to playing in the NFL and announcing games, he had also earned an accounting degree and a law degree. She liked that he was so athletic, likeable, and smart. These were all qualities she strived for herself.

"Maybe I am a little biased. I bet Cris Collinsworth would be good at the Great Debate," she said as the bus arrived at her stop. She grabbed her backpack and waited for the vehicle to come to a complete stop before standing.

"You're not too bad at it yourself, Scarlet," Mr. V said as she stepped off the bus. "Let's have a round of applause for Scarlet, everyone." She smiled as the bus pulled away with her classmates still clapping and cheering. Mr. V was a very impressive person himself, she thought.

CHAPTER TWO

SON of a BASKETBALL PLAYER

Anthony Cris Collinsworth was born in Dayton, Ohio, on January 27, 1959. His parents, Abe and Donetta, never called their first child by his first name, though. Cris has said that they wanted to name him Cris Anthony. But they worried that placing the names in that order made them sound like the flower called a chrysanthemum.

CHAPTER TWO

Abe's full name was Abraham Lincoln Collinsworth. His parents named him after the beloved sixteenth president of the United States. Abe was born on Lincoln's birthday. Abe had been a talented basketball player when he was a young man. He played both in high school and at the University of Kentucky. Cris proudly says that people would show up to his father's college games early just to watch him slam-dunk balls during practice.

After college, Abe coached basketball. He was coaching a game at Kings Mills High School when Donetta went into labor with Cris. By the time the game was over, Abe had become a father. The family often joked that the story of Abe missing the birth of his first son because of a basketball game showed how important sports were in the Collinsworth household.

SON of a BASKETBALL PLAYER

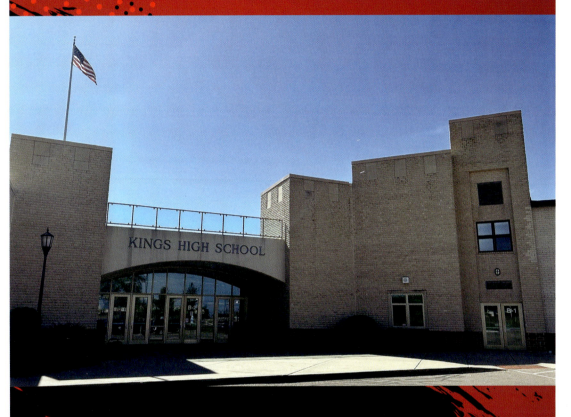

The Ohio high school where Abe Collinsworth coached basketball was replaced by Kings High School in 1967. The new school was built to serve students from Kings Mills and several other nearby districts.

CHAPTER **TWO**

Cris was a little too proud of the medal he won for being the fastest student in his class.

SON of a BASKETBALL PLAYER

When Cris was four years old, his family moved from Ohio to Florida. His parents, who were both teachers, settled in Eau Gallie. Cris and his two brothers grew up in this neighborhood, which is now part of Melbourne. Both Abe and Donetta taught their sons to be humble. But Cris didn't always listen.

When he was in the third grade, Cris won a medal one day for running faster than all the other students in his class. He went straight home to tell his mother how fast he was. When she warned him not to brag too much, Cris insisted that it wasn't bragging if what he was saying was true. Donetta decided that it was time to teach her son an important lesson. After taking him outdoors and measuring 50 yards, she challenged Cris to a foot race against her.

Cris told the story during an interview in *Sports Illustrated* years later. "I was laughing. C'mon, Mom, get serious,'" he recalled saying to her. "She beat me three straight [times]. I swear. You don't mess around with Mom," he added.

CHAPTER **TWO**

Cris entered Titusville's Astronaut High School in 1972. The school was given this name because it is so close to the Kennedy Space Center. Cris's interest in athletics had only increased by this time. He focused much of his effort on basketball. He told the *Sports Business Journal*, "I literally went to basketball camp for nine weeks every summer, and after a while, you get pretty good at it."

In addition to basketball, Cris played football and ran on the school's track team. His speed made him stand out in all three sports. But as time went on, it was football that brought him the most attention. As a senior, Cris was named an All-American quarterback by four different publications. When the time came for college, the University of Florida offered Cris a football **scholarship**. He headed there soon after graduating from Astronaut High School in 1977.

SON of a BASKETBALL PLAYER

Astronaut High School's name makes the institution sound like a place students learn about space travel. But the name actually came from the school's location.

CHAPTER THREE

FROM A QUARTERBACK to a TOP WIDE RECEIVER

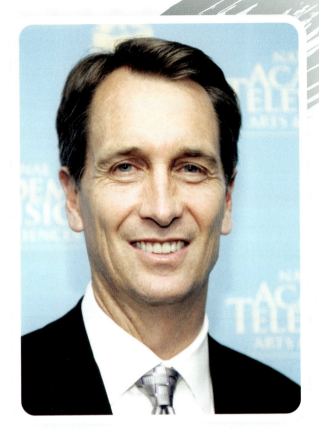

Cris started strong as a quarterback for the University of Florida Gators. During his first college football game, he threw a 99-yard pass. When fellow Gator Derrick Gaffney caught the ball, the two teammates tied the record for the longest pass completion in NCAA history. It looked like Cris's college football career as a quarterback was moving forward quickly. But an injury changed his direction.

CHAPTER **THREE**

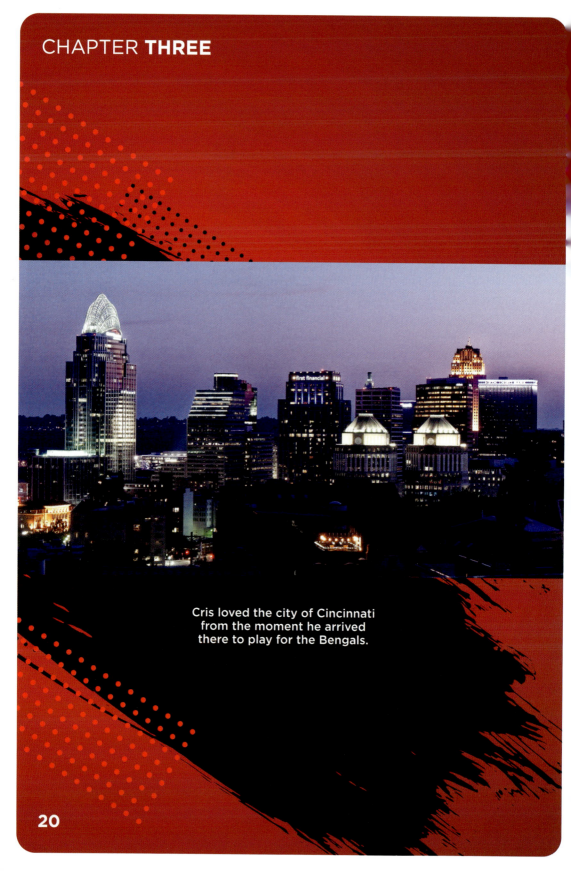

Cris loved the city of Cincinnati from the moment he arrived there to play for the Bengals.

FROM A QUARTERBACK to a TOP WIDE RECEIVER

After breaking his hand during his freshman year, Cris was moved to a different position on the football field. Coach Doug Dickey decided to see how Cris performed as a **wide receiver**. The move made him one of the most reliable wide receivers in college football for the next three seasons. He had found his calling playing this position. He scored 14 touchdowns in his time at the University of Florida. He caught 120 passes for 1,937 yards. He was named Most Valuable Player of the Tangerine Bowl, his final college game.

The 1981 NFL Draft brought Cris back to Ohio. The Cincinnati Bengals chose him in the second round of the annual event. Cris told *Cincinnati Magazine* he felt a rush of **adrenaline** just looking at the city's downtown skyline as he arrived. "I remember driving my Mercury Bobcat to training camp and coming down the cut in the hill on I-75 for the first time and seeing the bridges and the city revealed and almost overwhelmed me."

CHAPTER THREE

His nerves didn't stop him from succeeding in his new role as a professional football player. Just as he had done in college, he started his NFL career off with a bang. He wasted no time in becoming the Bengals' top receiver. He set the team's rookie record with 67 receptions. No rookie receiver in the entire NFL had reached this number in more than two decades.

In the NFL, Cris continued to be known for his speed. Sports journalists joked that he had wheels. At 6'5" tall with a thin build, his size made it difficult for opponents to block him from catching the ball.

The Bengals made it all the way to the Super Bowl in Cris's first season with the team. It was the first time the team had ever played in the big game. They went up against the San Francisco 49ers on January 24, 1982. Although the Bengals ended up losing Super Bowl XVI, announcers described Cris's performance in the big game as incredible. He had 5 receptions for 107 yards. But he fumbled the ball at a crucial moment that led San Francisco to start a touchdown drive.

FROM A QUARTERBACK to a TOP WIDE RECEIVER

Cris quickly became a valuable player to the Bengals. During his rookie season, he helped them get all the way to the Super Bowl.

CHAPTER **THREE**

Cris went on to play for Cincinnati for seven more seasons. In his final season, the team made it into the Super Bowl a second time. It seemed like a chance for Cris to go out on top. But he caught just 3 passes for 40 scoreless yards in the game. The Bengals lost to the 49ers again in Super Bowl XXIII.

Cris felt devastated that he missed his second chance at the Vince Lombardi trophy. In 2022, the *Los Angeles Times* asked him about how he felt about his two Super Bowl appearances. He replied, "It's obviously a **résumé** kind of thing to say you were in two Super Bowls, but the reality of it is, I've never watched either game. . . . Just can't make myself watch either one."

FROM A QUARTERBACK to a TOP WIDE RECEIVER

Super Bowl XXIII marked Cris's final performance as an NFL player. Joe Montana led the San Francisco 49ers in their defeat of the Bengals in the game.

CHAPTER FOUR

BEST LAID PLANS

With his NFL career behind him, Cris needed a new career path. WLW, a radio station in Cincinnati, asked him to fill in as the host of a sports program. Cris agreed. But he didn't see broadcasting as his future. Instead, he decided that he would put the accounting degree he had earned at the University of Florida to use. But he didn't want to work as an accountant either. He chose to add another degree to his résumé and become a tax law attorney. Thinking ahead, he had started attending the University of Cincinnati's College of Law before he finished playing football.

CHAPTER **FOUR**

Cris took other broadcasting jobs to make some extra money while he was completing his law degree. He told the *Minneapolis Star-Tribune*, "I had no idea what I was doing when I started." But his inexperience didn't stop him from succeeding in the business. In 1989, HBO's *Inside the NFL* offered him a job reporting feature stories for the program. Next, NBC gave him work as an **analyst** for a few college and NFL games.

He still wasn't counting on supporting himself solely with broadcasting work, though. In addition to his tax law plan, Cris bought a night club in Cincinnati as an investment. When friends asked to set him up on a blind date, he suggested that he and the young woman named Holly meet at this club he'd named the Precinct. Although they attended the same law school, Cris and Holly hadn't met until now. Their friends were right to believe they would get along well. The couple soon married and bought a home near the Ohio River. They went on to have four children together—Jack, Ashley, Austin, and Katie.

Best LAID PLANS

Inside The NFL featured sports broadcasters (left to right) Len Dawson, Jerry Glanville, Cris Collinsworth, and Nick Buoniconti.

CHAPTER **FOUR**

Holly stuck with her plan of practicing law as Cris dove deeper into his new career in sports broadcasting.

Cris's résumé was now expanding with his growing experience. Although he earned his law degree in 1991, he didn't end up using it like Holly did. As she began practicing law, he dove deeper into work as an on-air personality. Soon, he had done commentary for NBC, Fox, and the NFL Network.

In 2009, NBC made him his biggest offer in broadcasting yet—the chance to host *Sunday Night Football*. He agreed, cementing himself in his new career that he never expected to last. But others likely suspected that he would stick around even if Cris hadn't. NBC producer Fred Gaudelli always saw Cris as a professional broadcaster. Gaudelli told the *Star-Tribune*, "He's not an ex-football player doing television, he's a television broadcaster who happens to be an ex-football player."

CHAPTER **FOUR**

Best **LAID PLANS**

Cris has met many football legends during his broadcasting career. Two were former NFL quarterbacks Roger Staubach (second from left) and Troy Aikman (third from left).

CHAPTER FIVE

SUNDAY NIGHT FOOTBALL

John Madden (left) and Al Michaels (center) with Cris

Cris began his work on *Sunday Night Football* alongside Al Michaels, taking over for broadcasting legend John Madden. Many people had assumed that Cris would become Madden's replacement. Years after Cris took over the role, Madden told him that he had decided to retire after attending a birthday party for Cris. When Madden realized that Cris was turning fifty, the senior broadcaster decided he had held the job long enough. He thought it was time to give the younger broadcaster his chance.

35

CHAPTER **FIVE**

As excited as Cris was to take on his new role, he also wasn't in a rush. As a father, he wanted to be in the stands cheering his kids on in their own athletic pursuits. As he began his *Sunday Night Football* duties, one of Cris's sons was playing football for Notre Dame while the other was on his high school team. Cris's previous work schedule made it much easier for him to attend their games. He joked with a journalist from the *Awful Announcing* website, "[Madden] really could have done me a favor by staying there a couple more years."

But Cris was a natural at calling games with Michaels. The two men bonded over their mutual love of football. And each broadcaster brought a unique perspective to the program each week. While Michaels had a journalism background, he respected the things Cris noticed about the game that only a former player might. In an interview with *Parade*, Michaels shared, "Cris sees stuff inside the plays I wouldn't think of in a hundred years. You think it's about what a wide receiver did, and Cris will show you it's all about the right tackle."

SUNDAY NIGHT FOOTBALL

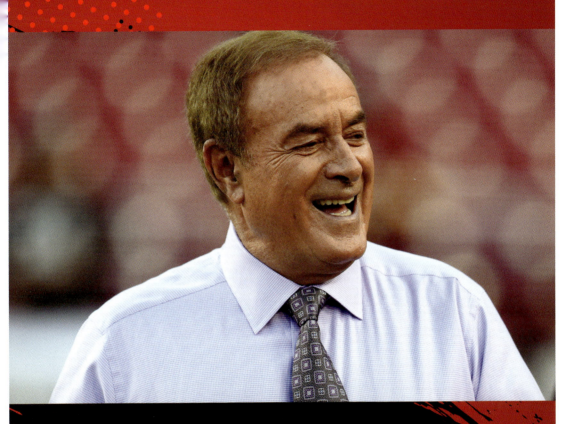

With their differing backgrounds, Al Michaels and Cris offered a well-rounded perspective of the games they announced together.

CHAPTER **FIVE**

Mike Tirico and Cris had been calling games together for a while when Tirico became Cris's new cohost for *Sunday Night Football*.

SUNDAY NIGHT FOOTBALL

The pair continued announcing games together for the next 13 football seasons. Along the way, Cris racked up more than a dozen Sports Emmy Awards. He has also been **inducted** into the Sports Broadcasting Hall of Fame.

In 2022, Cris performed in a Super Bowl that included Cincinnati. The Bengals had once again made it into the top game in the NFL. But this time instead of playing, Cris was calling the game. His beloved Bengals put in a good effort even though they lost the game to the Los Angeles Rams with a final score of 23 to 20.

That same year, Mike Tirico took over announcing for Al Michaels on *Sunday Night Football*. Viewers already knew that Tirico and Cris had good on-air chemistry. They had called twenty games together during their careers. Fans hope the pair will continue working together on the program for many more seasons.

CHAPTER **FIVE**

In addition to the many awards Cris has won as an announcer, he has also won a great deal of respect from his colleagues. *Sunday Night Football* producer Rob Hyland told the Sports Broadcasters Hall of Fame, "Cris is one of the most honest and fearless broadcasters of our generation. He is curious, thoughtful, and has a great sense of humor, which all play into his unique ability to make football's most complicated **intricacies** understandable and enjoyable for 20 million people every Sunday night."

SUNDAY NIGHT FOOTBALL

After an impressive career in the NFL, Cris has become one of the most successful sports broadcasters on the air today.

TIMELINE

1959   Anthony Cris Collinsworth is born in Dayton, Ohio, on January 27.

1963   He moves with his family to the city in Florida now known as Melbourne.

1976   He is named an All-American Quarterback by four publications.

1977   Cris graduates from Astronaut High School in Titusville, Florida.

He accepts a scholarship to play college football at the University of Florida.

1978   A coach at the University of Florida moves Cris to the position of wide receiver.

1981   Cris graduates from college with an accounting degree.

He begins his professional football career with the Cincinnati Bengals.

1982   Cris plays in his first Super Bowl. The Bengals lose the game to the San Francisco 49ers.

1989   Cris is devastated when Cincinnati loses its second Super Bowl to San Francisco.

He decides to retire from the NFL.

1991   Cris earns a law degree that he plans to use as a tax law attorney. But his part-time job as an announcer takes him in a different direction.

2009   He is offered the job of co-host of *Sunday Night Football*. He replaces the legendary John Madden on the program.

2022   Cris returns to the Super Bowl with the Cincinnati Bengals on the field. He announces their games against the Los Angeles Rams, who win.

2023   He is inducted into the Sports Broadcasting Hall of Fame.

FIND OUT MORE

PRINT

Coleman, Ted. *Cincinnati Bengals*. Mendota Heights, MN: Press Box Books, 2022.

Frederickson, Kevin. *Wide Receivers*. Minnetonka, MN: North Star Editions, 2019.

Gagne, Tammy. *Nate Burleson*. Hallandale, FL: Mitchell Lane Publishers, 2024.

ON THE INTERNET

Cincinnati Bengals
www.bengals.com

Sports Broadcasting Hal of Fame
www.sportsbroadcastinghalloffame.org

Sunday Night Football
www.nbcsports.com/nfl/snf

GLOSSARY

adrenaline
A hormone that causes feelings of heightened energy or excitement

analyst
A person who offers commentary based on expert insight

context
Surrounding information that helps make the meaning of a sentence or sentences clearer

inducted
Admitted as a member

intricacies
Complex details

quarterback
A football player who leads a team's offense by throwing passes or running with the ball

résumé
A list of skills and job experience given to a prospective employer

scholarship
A financial award granted to a student to help pay for further education

wide receiver
A football player positioned on the offensive side of the field who catches passes from the quarterback

WORKS CONSULTED

"Astronaut High's Cris Collinsworth: Winner of Multiple Emmy Awards, NFL Pro Bowler," *Space Coast Daily*, January 16, 2017. https://spacecoastdaily.com/2017/01/astronaut-highs-cris-collinsworth-winner-of-multiple-emmy-awards-nfl-pro-bowler.

Broyles, Ryan. "Did Cris Collinsworth Play for the Bengals?" *Pro Football Network*, November 5, 2023. https://www.profootballnetwork.com/did-cris-collinsworth-play-for-bengals-lifestyle/#:~:text=Florida%20coach%20Doug%20Dickey%20moved,Head%20Ball%20Coach%E2%80%9D%20Steve%20Spurrier.

Farmer, Sam. "Q&A: Cris Collinsworth Recalls Tortuous Super Bowl Losses with Bengals, Who Get Third Try," *Los Angeles Times*, February 8, 2022. https://www.latimes.com/sports/story/2022-02-08/qa-cris-collinsworth-super-bowl-losses-bengals.

Harry, Chris. "On This Date in Gators' History: September 17, 1977," *Florida Gators*, n.d. https://floridagators.com/news/2012/9/17/1046.

Hernandez, Kristian. "Sports Broadcasting Hall of Fame 2023: Cris Collinsworth the Familiar Football Analyst in Primetime," *Sports Video Group*, November 21, 2023. https://www.sportsvideo.org/2023/11/21/sports-broadcasting-hall-of-fame-2023-cris-collinsworth-the-familiar-football-analyst-in-primetime/#:~:text=With%20his%20prowess%20on%20the,of%20Florida%20in%20Gainesville%2C%20FL.

Madkour, Abraham D. "Collinsworth's Constant Quest for What's Next," *Sports Business Journal*, August 31, 2015. https://www.sportsbusinessjournal.com/Journal/Issues/2015/08/31/Opinion/Catching-Up-with-Cris-Collinsworth.aspx.

Marchand, Andrew. "Cris Collinsworth's Third Bengals Super Bowl Comes in the NBC Booth," *New York Post*, February 7, 2022. https://nypost.com/2022/02/07/super-bowl-2022-ex-bengal-cris-collinsworth-to-call-game.

Steinberg, Brian. "Miki Tirico Joins NBC's '*Sunday Night Football*' Booth in Latest Sports Talent Maneuver," *Variety*, March 22, 2022. https://variety.com/2022/tv/news/mike-tirico-sunday-night-football-nbc-joins-1235211953.

Thames, Alanis. "Super Bowl: How the Rams Beat the Bengals to Win the Super Bowl," *The New York Times*, February 13, 2022. https://www.nytimes.com/live/2022/02/13/sports/super-bowl-rams-bengals#:~:text=The%20Rams%20clinch%20the%20Super,final%20stop%20of%20Joe%20Burrow.&text=INGLEWOOD%2C%20Calif.,on%20Sunday%2C%20capturing%20an%20N.F.L.

Underwood, John. "Catch a Rising Star," *Sports Illustrated*, December 14, 1981. https://vault.si.com/vault/1981/12/14/catch-a-catching-star-give-a-listen-to-cincinnatis-rookie-sensation-cris-collinsworth-who-can-drop-a-quote-as-well-as-he-can-grab-a-pass.

Vadala, Nick. "Eagles Have Filed for a Trademark on the 'Brotherly Shove,'" *The Philadelphia Enquirer*, October 17, 2023. https://www.inquirer.com/news/brotherly-shove-philadelphia-eagles-trademark-merchandise-20231017.html#:~:text=Known%20more%20generically%20as%20the,soon%20after%20the%20play%20begins.

INDEX

Astronaut High School, 16
Cincinnati Bengals, 21, 22, 39
Collinsworth, Abe, 11, 12, 15
Collinsworth, Ashley, 28
Collinsworth, Austin, 28
Collinsworth, Cris
  awards, 39
  birth, 11, 12
  childhood, 11–16
  education, 16, 19–21
  records, 19, 22
Collinsworth, Donetta, 11, 12, 15
Collinsworth, Holly, 28, 31
Collinsworth, Jack, 28
Collinsworth, Katie, 28
Dickey, Doug, 21
Madden, John, 35, 36
Michaels, Al, 36, 39
NFL Draft, 21
quarterback, 16, 19
Sports Broadcasting Hall of Fame, 39
Sunday Night Football, 35–40
Super Bowl XVI, 22
Super Bowl LVI, 39
Tirico, Mike, 39
University of Cincinnati College of Law, 27
University of Florida, 16, 19, 21, 27
wide receiver, 21, 36

ABOUT THE AUTHOR

Tammy Gagne is a freelance writer and editor who specializes in educational nonfiction for young people. She has written hundreds of books on a wide range of topics. Some of her favorite projects have been about journalists and athletes. Tammy's other books in the Award-Winning Broadcasters series include *Malika Andrews* **and** *Mike Tirico.*